This is the Ancestry of:

If you want to understand today,
you have to search yesterday.

-Pearl S. Buck

Our Story:

Our Story:

Our Story:

Our Story:

Our Story:

Our Family

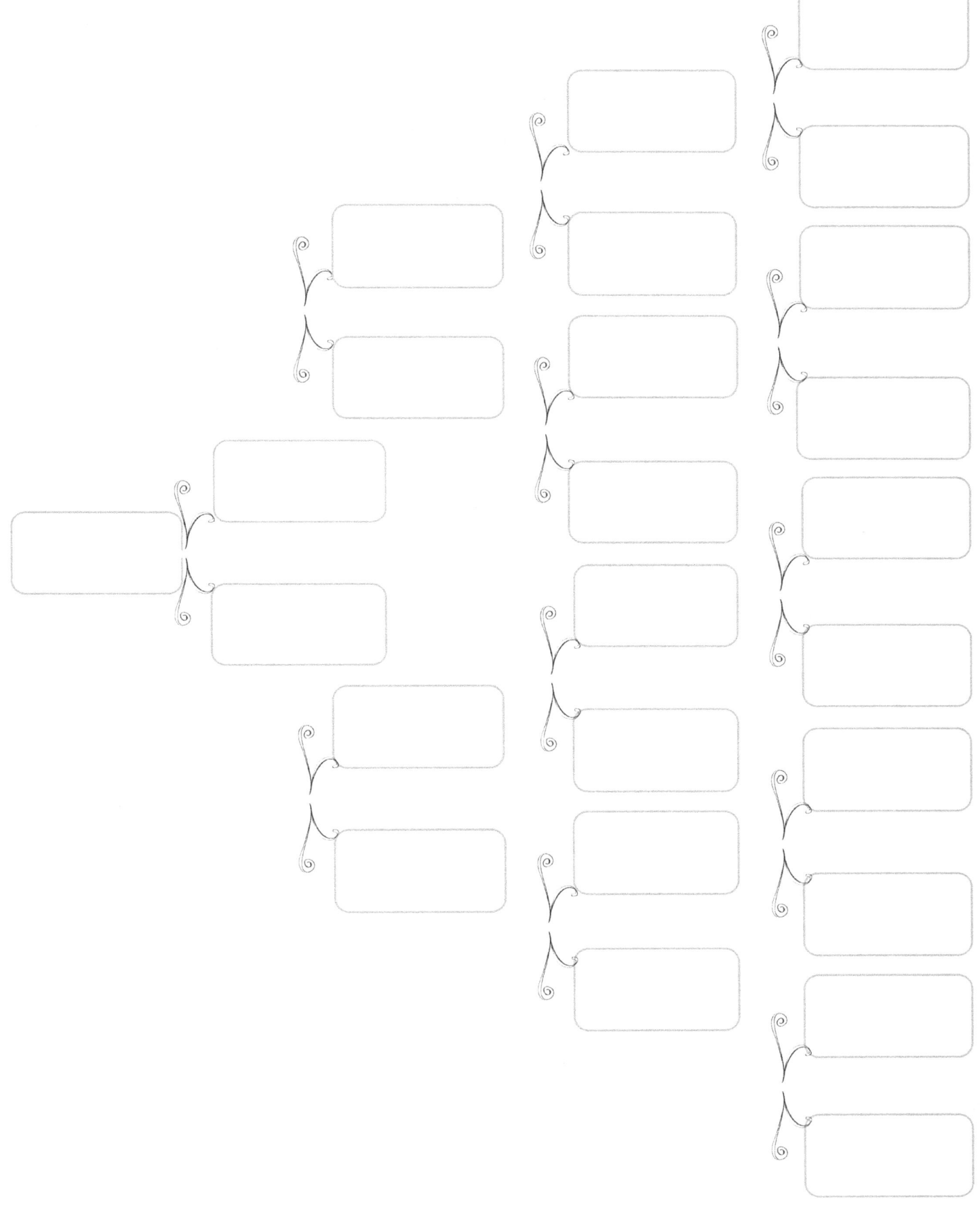

Our Family

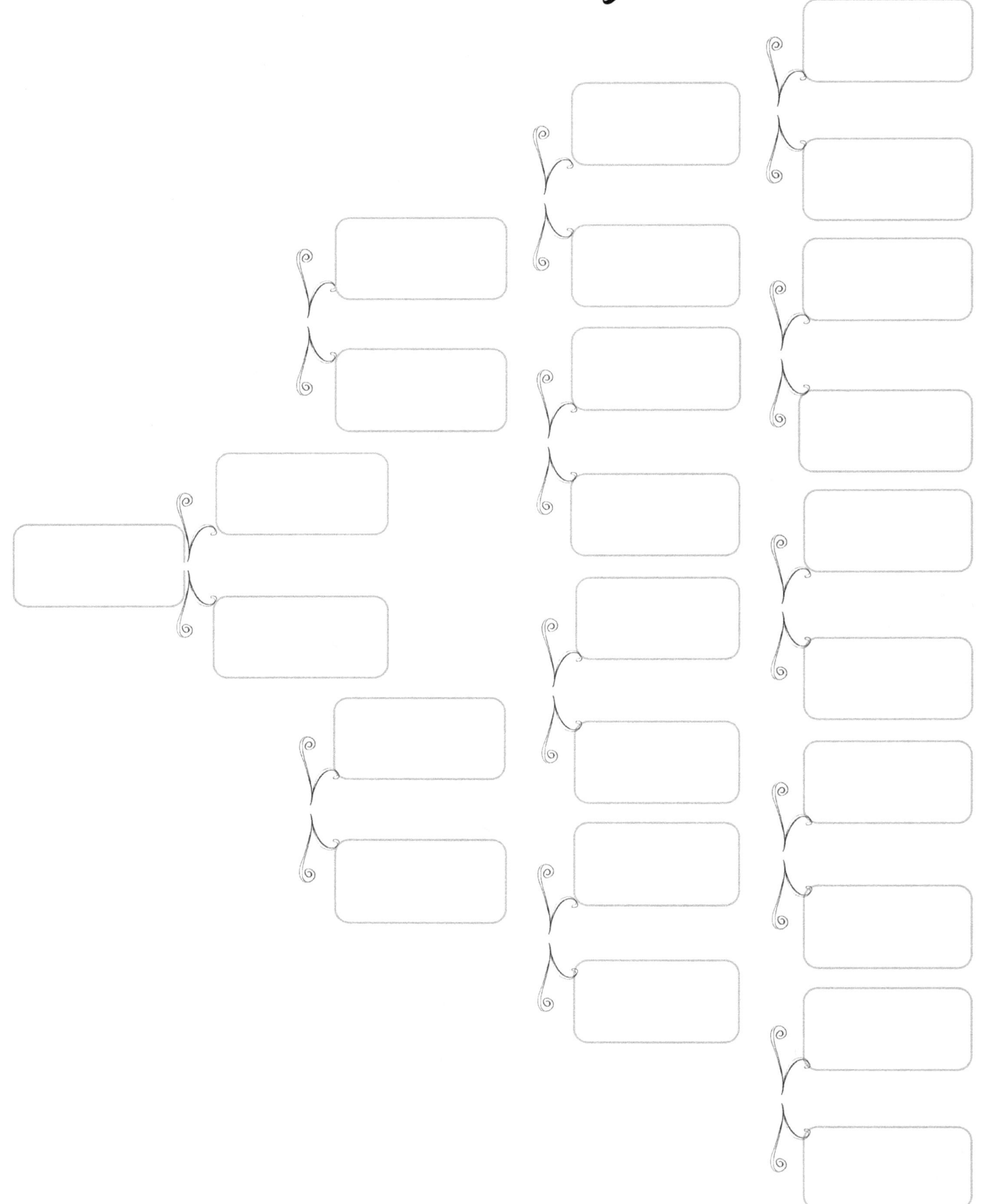

Our Family

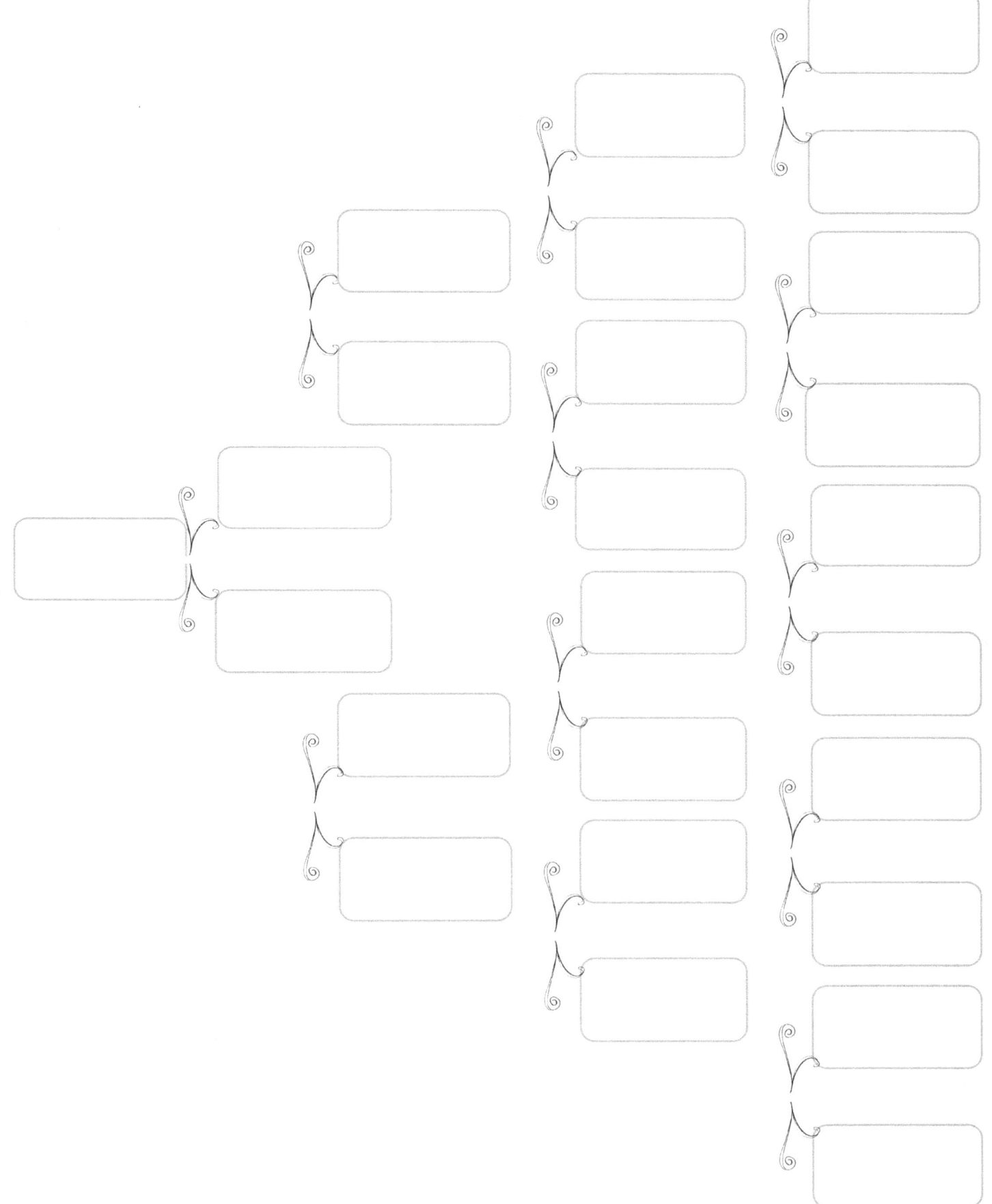

Ancestor's Full Name: _____

Relationship: _____ ☐ Paternal ☐ Maternal

Date of Birth: _____ Birthplace: _____ Date of Death: _____

Parents

Marriages

Date: _____ Spouse: _____

Date: _____ Spouse: _____

Date: _____ Spouse: _____

Date: _____ Spouse: _____

Siblings

Children

Name	DOB	Name	DOB
Name	DOB	Name	DOB
Name	DOB	Name	DOB
Name	DOB	Name	DOB
Name	DOB	Name	DOB
Name	DOB	Name	DOB
Name	DOB	Name	DOB
Name	DOB	Name	DOB

Source of Information

Birth Certificate

Death Certificate

Marriage Certificate

Obituary

Grave Marker

Census

Will/Probate Records

Ancestry DNA

Newspaper Article

23 & Me

Deeds/Land Records

Military Records

Google/Internet

Other

Leads

Notes

Notes

Timeline of Life Events

Ancestor's Full Name: _____

Relationship: _____   ☐ Paternal   ☐ Maternal

Date of Birth: _____   Birthplace: _____   Date of Death: _____

Parents

Marriages

Date: Spouse:

Date: Spouse:

Date: Spouse:

Date: Spouse:

Siblings

Name	DOB
Name	DOB
Name	DOB
Name	DOB
Name	DOB
Name	DOB
Name	DOB
Name	DOB

Children

Name	DOB
Name	DOB
Name	DOB
Name	DOB
Name	DOB
Name	DOB
Name	DOB
Name	DOB

Source of Information

Birth Certificate

Death Certificate

Marriage Certificate

Obituary

Grave Marker

Census

Will/Probate Records

Ancestry DNA

Newspaper Article

23 & Me

Deeds/Land Records

Military Records

Google/Internet

Other

Leads

Notes

Notes

Timeline of Life Events

Ancestor's Full Name: _____

Relationship: _____ ☐ Paternal ☐ Maternal

Date of Birth: _____ Birthplace: _____ Date of Death: _____

Parents

Marriages

Date: _____ Spouse: _____

Date: _____ Spouse: _____

Date: _____ Spouse: _____

Date: _____ Spouse: _____

Siblings

Children

Name	DOB	Name	DOB
Name	DOB	Name	DOB
Name	DOB	Name	DOB
Name	DOB	Name	DOB
Name	DOB	Name	DOB
Name	DOB	Name	DOB
Name	DOB	Name	DOB
Name	DOB	Name	DOB
Name	DOB	Name	DOB

Source of Information

Birth Certificate

Death Certificate

Marriage Certificate

Obituary

Grave Marker

Census

Will/Probate Records

Ancestry DNA

Newspaper Article

23 & Me

Deeds/Land Records

Military Records

Google/Internet

Other

Leads

Notes

Notes

Timeline of Life Events

Ancestor's Full Name:

Relationship: _____ ☐ Paternal ☐ Maternal

Date of Birth: _____ Birthplace: _____ Date of Death: _____

Parents

Marriages

Date: _____ Spouse: _____

Date: _____ Spouse: _____

Date: _____ Spouse: _____

Date: _____ Spouse: _____

Siblings

Children

Name	DOB	Name	DOB
Name	DOB	Name	DOB
Name	DOB	Name	DOB
Name	DOB	Name	DOB
Name	DOB	Name	DOB
Name	DOB	Name	DOB
Name	DOB	Name	DOB
Name	DOB	Name	DOB

Source of Information

Birth Certificate

Death Certificate

Marriage Certificate

Obituary

Grave Marker

Census

Will/Probate Records

Ancestry DNA

Newspaper Article

23 & Me

Deeds/Land Records

Military Records

Google/Internet

Other

Leads

Notes

Notes

Timeline of Life Events

Ancestor's Full Name: _____

Relationship: _____ ☐ Paternal ☐ Maternal

Date of Birth: _____ Birthplace: _____ Date of Death: _____

Parents

Marriages

Date: _____ Spouse: _____

Date: _____ Spouse: _____

Date: _____ Spouse: _____

Date: _____ Spouse: _____

Siblings

Children

Name	DOB	Name	DOB
Name	DOB	Name	DOB
Name	DOB	Name	DOB
Name	DOB	Name	DOB
Name	DOB	Name	DOB
Name	DOB	Name	DOB
Name	DOB	Name	DOB
Name	DOB	Name	DOB
Name	DOB	Name	DOB

Source of Information

Birth Certificate

Death Certificate

Marriage Certificate

Obituary

Grave Marker

Census

Will/Probate Records

Ancestry DNA

Newspaper Article

23 & Me

Deeds/Land Records

Military Records

Google/Internet

Other

Leads

Notes

Notes

Timeline of Life Events

Ancestor's Full Name:

Relationship: _____ ☐ Paternal ☐ Maternal

Date of Birth: _____ **Birthplace:** _____ **Date of Death:** _____

Parents

Marriages

Date: Spouse:

Date: Spouse:

Date: Spouse:

Date: Spouse:

Siblings

Children

Name	DOB	Name	DOB
Name	DOB	Name	DOB
Name	DOB	Name	DOB
Name	DOB	Name	DOB
Name	DOB	Name	DOB
Name	DOB	Name	DOB
Name	DOB	Name	DOB
Name	DOB	Name	DOB
Name	DOB	Name	DOB

Source of Information

Birth Certificate

Death Certificate

Marriage Certificate

Obituary

Grave Marker

Census

Will/Probate Records

Ancestry DNA

Newspaper Article

23 & Me

Deeds/Land Records

Military Records

Google/Internet

Other

Leads

Notes

Notes

Timeline of Life Events

Ancestor's Full Name: _____

Relationship: _____ ☐ Paternal ☐ Maternal

Date of Birth: _____ Birthplace: _____ Date of Death: _____

Parents

Marriages

Date: Spouse:

Date: Spouse:

Date: Spouse:

Date: Spouse:

Siblings

Children

Name	DOB	Name	DOB
Name	DOB	Name	DOB
Name	DOB	Name	DOB
Name	DOB	Name	DOB
Name	DOB	Name	DOB
Name	DOB	Name	DOB
Name	DOB	Name	DOB
Name	DOB	Name	DOB
Name	DOB	Name	DOB

Source of Information

Birth Certificate

Death Certificate

Marriage Certificate

Obituary

Grave Marker

Census

Will/Probate Records

Ancestry DNA

Newspaper Article

23 & Me

Deeds/Land Records

Military Records

Google/Internet

Other

Leads

Notes

Notes

Timeline of Life Events

Ancestor's Full Name: _____

Relationship: _____ ☐ Paternal ☐ Maternal

Date of Birth: _____ Birthplace: _____ Date of Death: _____

Parents

Marriages

Date: _____ Spouse: _____

Date: _____ Spouse: _____

Date: _____ Spouse: _____

Date: _____ Spouse: _____

Siblings

Children

Name	DOB	Name	DOB
Name	DOB	Name	DOB
Name	DOB	Name	DOB
Name	DOB	Name	DOB
Name	DOB	Name	DOB
Name	DOB	Name	DOB
Name	DOB	Name	DOB
Name	DOB	Name	DOB
Name	DOB	Name	DOB

Source of Information

Birth Certificate

Death Certificate

Marriage Certificate

Obituary

Grave Marker

Census

Will/Probate Records

Ancestry DNA

Newspaper Article

23 & Me

Deeds/Land Records

Military Records

Google/Internet

Other

Leads

Notes

Notes

Timeline of Life Events

Ancestor's Full Name: _____

Relationship: _____ ☐ Paternal ☐ Maternal

Date of Birth: _____ Birthplace: _____ Date of Death: _____

Parents

Marriages

Date: _____ Spouse: _____

Date: _____ Spouse: _____

Date: _____ Spouse: _____

Date: _____ Spouse: _____

Siblings

Children

Name	DOB	Name	DOB
Name	DOB	Name	DOB
Name	DOB	Name	DOB
Name	DOB	Name	DOB
Name	DOB	Name	DOB
Name	DOB	Name	DOB
Name	DOB	Name	DOB
Name	DOB	Name	DOB

Source of Information

Birth Certificate

Death Certificate

Marriage Certificate

Obituary

Grave Marker

Census

Will/Probate Records

Ancestry DNA

Newspaper Article

23 & Me

Deeds/Land Records

Military Records

Google/Internet

Other

Leads

Notes

Notes

Timeline of Life Events

Ancestor's Full Name: _____

Relationship: _____ ☐ Paternal ☐ Maternal

Date of Birth: _____ Birthplace: _____ Date of Death: _____

Parents

Marriages

Date: _____ Spouse: _____

Date: _____ Spouse: _____

Date: _____ Spouse: _____

Date: _____ Spouse: _____

Siblings

Children

Name	DOB	Name	DOB
Name	DOB	Name	DOB
Name	DOB	Name	DOB
Name	DOB	Name	DOB
Name	DOB	Name	DOB
Name	DOB	Name	DOB
Name	DOB	Name	DOB
Name	DOB	Name	DOB

Source of Information

Birth Certificate

Death Certificate

Marriage Certificate

Obituary

Grave Marker

Census

Will/Probate Records

Ancestry DNA

Newspaper Article

23 & Me

Deeds/Land Records

Military Records

Google/Internet

Other

Leads

Notes

Notes

Timeline of Life Events

Ancestor's Full Name: _____

Relationship: _____ ☐ Paternal ☐ Maternal

Date of Birth: _____ Birthplace: _____ Date of Death: _____

Parents

Marriages

Date: _____ Spouse: _____

Date: _____ Spouse: _____

Date: _____ Spouse: _____

Date: _____ Spouse: _____

Siblings

Children

Name	DOB	Name	DOB
Name	DOB	Name	DOB
Name	DOB	Name	DOB
Name	DOB	Name	DOB
Name	DOB	Name	DOB
Name	DOB	Name	DOB
Name	DOB	Name	DOB
Name	DOB	Name	DOB
Name	DOB	Name	DOB

Source of Information

Birth Certificate

Death Certificate

Marriage Certificate

Obituary

Grave Marker

Census

Will/Probate Records

Ancestry DNA

Newspaper Article

23 & Me

Deeds/Land Records

Military Records

Google/Internet

Other

Leads

Notes

Notes

Timeline of Life Events

Ancestor's Full Name:

Relationship: _____ ☐ Paternal   ☐ Maternal

Date of Birth: _____ Birthplace: _____ Date of Death: _____

Parents

Marriages

Date: _____   Spouse: _____

Date: _____   Spouse: _____

Date: _____   Spouse: _____

Date: _____   Spouse: _____

Siblings

Children

Name	DOB	Name	DOB
Name	DOB	Name	DOB
Name	DOB	Name	DOB
Name	DOB	Name	DOB
Name	DOB	Name	DOB
Name	DOB	Name	DOB
Name	DOB	Name	DOB
Name	DOB	Name	DOB

Source of Information

Birth Certificate

Death Certificate

Marriage Certificate

Obituary

Grave Marker

Census

Will/Probate Records

Ancestry DNA

Newspaper Article

23 & Me

Deeds/Land Records

Military Records

Google/Internet

Other

Leads

Notes

Notes

Timeline of Life Events

Ancestor's Full Name: _____

Relationship: _____ ☐ Paternal ☐ Maternal

Date of Birth: _____ Birthplace: _____ Date of Death: _____

Parents

Marriages

Date: _____ Spouse: _____

Date: _____ Spouse: _____

Date: _____ Spouse: _____

Date: _____ Spouse: _____

Siblings

Children

Name	DOB	Name	DOB
Name	DOB	Name	DOB
Name	DOB	Name	DOB
Name	DOB	Name	DOB
Name	DOB	Name	DOB
Name	DOB	Name	DOB
Name	DOB	Name	DOB
Name	DOB	Name	DOB

Source of Information

Birth Certificate

Death Certificate

Marriage Certificate

Obituary

Grave Marker

Census

Will/Probate Records

Ancestry DNA

Newspaper Article

23 & Me

Deeds/Land Records

Military Records

Google/Internet

Other

Leads

Notes

Notes

Timeline of Life Events

Ancestor's Full Name: _____

Relationship: _____ ☐ Paternal ☐ Maternal

Date of Birth: _____ Birthplace: _____ Date of Death: _____

Parents

Marriages

Date: _____ Spouse: _____

Date: _____ Spouse: _____

Date: _____ Spouse: _____

Date: _____ Spouse: _____

Siblings

Children

Name	DOB	Name	DOB
Name	DOB	Name	DOB
Name	DOB	Name	DOB
Name	DOB	Name	DOB
Name	DOB	Name	DOB
Name	DOB	Name	DOB
Name	DOB	Name	DOB
Name	DOB	Name	DOB
Name	DOB	Name	DOB

Source of Information

Birth Certificate

Death Certificate

Marriage Certificate

Obituary

Grave Marker

Census

Will/Probate Records

Ancestry DNA

Newspaper Article

23 & Me

Deeds/Land Records

Military Records

Google/Internet

Other

Leads

Notes

Notes

Timeline of Life Events

Ancestor's Full Name: _____

Relationship: _____ ☐ Paternal ☐ Maternal

Date of Birth: _____ Birthplace: _____ Date of Death: _____

Parents

Marriages

Date: _____ Spouse: _____

Date: _____ Spouse: _____

Date: _____ Spouse: _____

Date: _____ Spouse: _____

Siblings

Children

Name	DOB	Name	DOB
Name	DOB	Name	DOB
Name	DOB	Name	DOB
Name	DOB	Name	DOB
Name	DOB	Name	DOB
Name	DOB	Name	DOB
Name	DOB	Name	DOB
Name	DOB	Name	DOB

Source of Information

Birth Certificate

Death Certificate

Marriage Certificate

Obituary

Grave Marker

Census

Will/Probate Records

Ancestry DNA

Newspaper Article

23 & Me

Deeds/Land Records

Military Records

Google/Internet

Other

Leads

Notes

Notes

Timeline of Life Events

Ancestor's Full Name: _____

Relationship: _____ ☐ Paternal ☐ Maternal

Date of Birth: _____ Birthplace: _____ Date of Death: _____

Parents

Marriages

Date: _____ Spouse: _____

Date: _____ Spouse: _____

Date: _____ Spouse: _____

Date: _____ Spouse: _____

Siblings

Children

Name	DOB	Name	DOB
Name	DOB	Name	DOB
Name	DOB	Name	DOB
Name	DOB	Name	DOB
Name	DOB	Name	DOB
Name	DOB	Name	DOB
Name	DOB	Name	DOB
Name	DOB	Name	DOB
Name	DOB	Name	DOB

Source of Information

Birth Certificate

Death Certificate

Marriage Certificate

Obituary

Grave Marker

Census

Will/Probate Records

Ancestry DNA

Newspaper Article

23 & Me

Deeds/Land Records

Military Records

Google/Internet

Other

Leads

Notes

Notes

Timeline of Life Events

Ancestor's Full Name:

Relationship: _____ ☐ Paternal ☐ Maternal

Date of Birth: _____ Birthplace: _____ Date of Death: _____

Parents

Marriages

Date: _____ Spouse: _____

Date: _____ Spouse: _____

Date: _____ Spouse: _____

Date: _____ Spouse: _____

Siblings

Children

Name	DOB	Name	DOB
Name	DOB	Name	DOB
Name	DOB	Name	DOB
Name	DOB	Name	DOB
Name	DOB	Name	DOB
Name	DOB	Name	DOB
Name	DOB	Name	DOB
Name	DOB	Name	DOB

Source of Information

Birth Certificate

Death Certificate

Marriage Certificate

Obituary

Grave Marker

Census

Will/Probate Records

Ancestry DNA

Newspaper Article

23 & Me

Deeds/Land Records

Military Records

Google/Internet

Other

Leads

Notes

Notes

Timeline of Life Events

Ancestor's Full Name: _____

Relationship: _____ ☐ Paternal ☐ Maternal

Date of Birth: _____ Birthplace: _____ Date of Death: _____

Parents

Marriages

Date: _____ Spouse: _____

Date: _____ Spouse: _____

Date: _____ Spouse: _____

Date: _____ Spouse: _____

Siblings

Children

Name	DOB	Name	DOB
Name	DOB	Name	DOB
Name	DOB	Name	DOB
Name	DOB	Name	DOB
Name	DOB	Name	DOB
Name	DOB	Name	DOB
Name	DOB	Name	DOB
Name	DOB	Name	DOB
Name	DOB	Name	DOB

Source of Information

Birth Certificate

Death Certificate

Marriage Certificate

Obituary

Grave Marker

Census

Will/Probate Records

Ancestry DNA

Newspaper Article

23 & Me

Deeds/Land Records

Military Records

Google/Internet

Other

Leads

Notes

Notes

Timeline of Life Events

Ancestor's Full Name: _____

Relationship: _____ [ ] Paternal [ ] Maternal

Date of Birth: Birthplace: Date of Death:

Parents

Marriages

Date: Spouse:

Date: Spouse:

Date: Spouse:

Date: Spouse:

Siblings

Children

Name	DOB	Name	DOB
Name	DOB	Name	DOB
Name	DOB	Name	DOB
Name	DOB	Name	DOB
Name	DOB	Name	DOB
Name	DOB	Name	DOB
Name	DOB	Name	DOB
Name	DOB	Name	DOB

Source of Information

Birth Certificate

Death Certificate

Marriage Certificate

Obituary

Grave Marker

Census

Will/Probate Records

Ancestry DNA

Newspaper Article

23 & Me

Deeds/Land Records

Military Records

Google/Internet

Other

Leads

Notes

Notes

Timeline of Life Events

Ancestor's Full Name: _____

Relationship: _____ ☐ Paternal ☐ Maternal

Date of Birth: _____ Birthplace: _____ Date of Death: _____

Parents

Marriages

Date: _____ Spouse: _____

Date: _____ Spouse: _____

Date: _____ Spouse: _____

Date: _____ Spouse: _____

Siblings

Children

Name	DOB	Name	DOB
Name	DOB	Name	DOB
Name	DOB	Name	DOB
Name	DOB	Name	DOB
Name	DOB	Name	DOB
Name	DOB	Name	DOB
Name	DOB	Name	DOB
Name	DOB	Name	DOB
Name	DOB	Name	DOB

Source of Information

Birth Certificate

Death Certificate

Marriage Certificate

Obituary

Grave Marker

Census

Will/Probate Records

Ancestry DNA

Newspaper Article

23 & Me

Deeds/Land Records

Military Records

Google/Internet

Other

Leads

Notes

Notes

Timeline of Life Events

Ancestor's Full Name: _____

Relationship: _____ ☐ Paternal ☐ Maternal

Date of Birth: _____ Birthplace: _____ Date of Death: _____

Parents

Marriages

Date: Spouse:

Date: Spouse:

Date: Spouse:

Date: Spouse:

Siblings

Children

Name	DOB	Name	DOB
Name	DOB	Name	DOB
Name	DOB	Name	DOB
Name	DOB	Name	DOB
Name	DOB	Name	DOB
Name	DOB	Name	DOB
Name	DOB	Name	DOB
Name	DOB	Name	DOB

Source of Information

Birth Certificate

Death Certificate

Marriage Certificate

Obituary

Grave Marker

Census

Will/Probate Records

Ancestry DNA

Newspaper Article

23 & Me

Deeds/Land Records

Military Records

Google/Internet

Other

Leads

Notes

Notes

Timeline of Life Events

Ancestor's Full Name: _____

Relationship: _____ ☐ Paternal ☐ Maternal

Date of Birth: _____ Birthplace: _____ Date of Death: _____

Parents

Marriages

Date: _____ Spouse: _____

Date: _____ Spouse: _____

Date: _____ Spouse: _____

Date: _____ Spouse: _____

Siblings

Children

Name	DOB	Name	DOB
Name	DOB	Name	DOB
Name	DOB	Name	DOB
Name	DOB	Name	DOB
Name	DOB	Name	DOB
Name	DOB	Name	DOB
Name	DOB	Name	DOB
Name	DOB	Name	DOB
Name	DOB	Name	DOB

Source of Information

Birth Certificate

Death Certificate

Marriage Certificate

Obituary

Grave Marker

Census

Will/Probate Records

Ancestry DNA

Newspaper Article

23 & Me

Deeds/Land Records

Military Records

Google/Internet

Other

Leads

Notes

Notes

Timeline of Life Events

Ancestor's Full Name: _____

Relationship: _____ ☐ Paternal ☐ Maternal

Date of Birth: _____ Birthplace: _____ Date of Death: _____

Parents

Marriages

Date: _____ Spouse: _____

Date: _____ Spouse: _____

Date: _____ Spouse: _____

Date: _____ Spouse: _____

Siblings

Children

Name	DOB	Name	DOB
Name	DOB	Name	DOB
Name	DOB	Name	DOB
Name	DOB	Name	DOB
Name	DOB	Name	DOB
Name	DOB	Name	DOB
Name	DOB	Name	DOB
Name	DOB	Name	DOB

Source of Information

Birth Certificate

Death Certificate

Marriage Certificate

Obituary

Grave Marker

Census

Will/Probate Records

Ancestry DNA

Newspaper Article

23 & Me

Deeds/Land Records

Military Records

Google/Internet

Other

Leads

Notes

Notes

Timeline of Life Events